MYSTE

OF THE ANCIENT WORLD

THE MAYAN ENIGMA

CONSTANCE CORTEZ

WEIDENFELD & NICOLSON
LONDON

Between the 3rd and 10th centuries AD the Maya civilization covered the vast area now comprising Guatemala, Belize, northern El Salvador and Honduras, and the south-eastern Mexican states of Tabasco, Yucatan and Quintana Roo. The topography of the area – from the dense tropical rain forests of the lowlands to the mountainous pine forests of the Highlands – make this a truly remarkable phenomenon.

*P**alenque as it appeared in an 1844 lithograph by the British artist and architect, Frederick Catherwood.*

The area is hot and humid with torrential rainfalls occurring part of the year and minimal amounts of rain the rest. Despite these harsh conditions, the Maya established huge city-states ruled over by semi-divine kings. These lords were given a mandate by the gods to maintain both earthly and cosmic order. Responsibilities towards divine ancestors, the gods, and towards one's descendants were maintained through ritualized warfare and religious observances. Nowhere is the mandate from the gods more evident than in the art of two of the greatest Maya cities, Palenque and Copán.

Palenque, Mexico

The ancient city of Palenque is located in the jungles of Chiapas, Mexico. Its strategic placement, at the juncture between the lowland and highland regions greatly facilitated trade with other Maya sites and enhanced Palenque's economic importance during the Classic Period. The ruins of great temples and palaces on either side of the narrow Otulum River attest to the economic wealth of the city during its zenith (600–750 AD). Over 1,000 years of rain have washed clean the sides of the limestone structures, leaving behind only bone-white masonry. Though hard to imagine, all the structures at Palenque were once covered with smooth plaster and brightly painted, the favoured hue being red. Here and there, traces of paint indicate the original palette of the ancient artists. Hieroglyphic texts carved into interior walls and under eaves recount war campaigns and the births and accessions of great monarchs. The city's florescence can be attributed to two kings: Pacal, who ruled between 615 and 683 AD, and his son, Chan Bahlum who ruled between 684 and 702.

The image of GIII, the jaguar god of the underworld, adorns this incense brazier from Palenque. Both copal (dried pine resin) and dried human blood were directed towards the gods in the form of burnt offerings.

*T**he Temple of
the Inscriptions
at Palenque was
constructed in the
7th century by Pacal
the Great as his
mortuary temple.***

Perhaps the most famous and certainly most prominent structure at the site is Pacal's mortuary pyramid, the Temple of the Inscriptions. This building derives its modern name from the continuous text running along the back wall of the temple at its summit. Each of the pyramid's nine tiers refers to a level of the watery Maya underworld known as Xibalba (pronounced, 'she-bal´-ba'). The entire structure can be understood as a 'world mountain', a place associated not only with death but with emergence and life. The temple on top of the pyramid was metaphorically conceived of as a cave, the entrance to the underworld. It seems appropriate, then, that the stuccoed surfaces of this monument were originally painted red, the colour of life-sustaining blood.

Although locals and travellers knew of the presence of the site for centuries, most of the ancient city remained covered under a densely woven shroud of vines and foliage until the late 1940s, when the Mexican archaeologist, Alberto Ruz Lhuillier began his painstaking removal of more than 1000 years of accumulated forest growth. During his excavation and reconsolidation of the Temple of the Inscriptions, Ruz discovered a series of holes in one of the slabs which made up the floor of the temple. Removal of this slab revealed an entrance to a rubble-filled stairway. From 1950 to 1952, Ruz and his men meticulously removed the rubble from the corbel-vaulted passageway. As they

R *econstruction of the crypt below*
the Temple of the Inscriptions.

MERLE GREENE
1980

progressed the excavators found caches of ceramic, jade, shell, and pearl offerings. Midway down the stairs, they uncovered the bones of half a dozen youths who had, presumably, been sacrificed in honour of the pyramid's main inhabitant.

By the summer of 1952, the workers had excavated the entire length of the internal stairway and had come to a dead end a little below plaza level. Further passage was blocked by a tightly fitted, huge triangular stone. Eventually the obstruction was dislodged and, to their surprise, the archaeologists found themselves gazing at one of the most spectacular burials ever discovered in the New World. The vaulted crypt measured 9 m in length, 4 m wide, and 7 m high and was located almost directly below the central axis of the pyramid, some 27.5 m below the floor of the temple. Light brought into the room revealed images of nine life-size 'attendants' stuccoed to the walls, their gazes directed towards a huge limestone sarcophagus. Were these attendants placed there to stand eternal vigil over the sarcophagus, or were they somehow associated with each of the nine levels of Xibalba?

Examination of the 4-metre-long rectangular sarcophagus revealed that its surface had been carefully carved on five of its six surfaces. The lid was rolled back to expose an uncharacteristically tall male skeleton who had been adorned with jade ornaments including a jade belt and necklace. In each of his hands, he held a large jade

The jade mask worn by the dead Pacal was one of many jade objects found inside the sarcophagus.

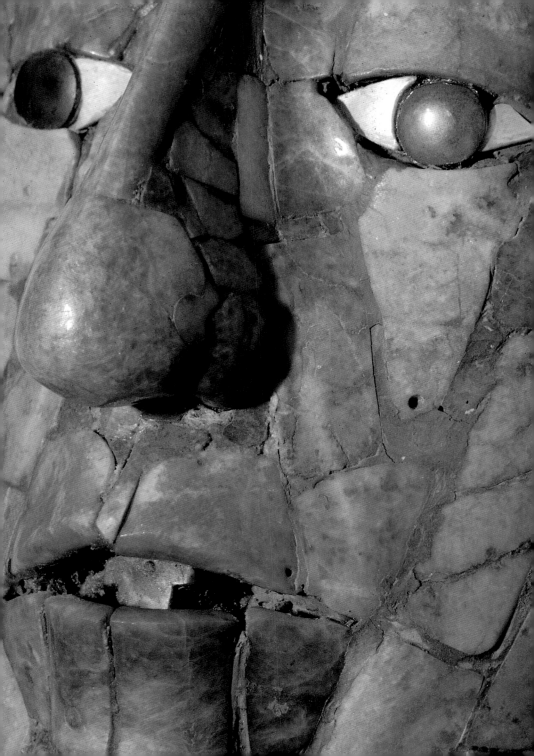

bead. After the removal of the jade mosaic mask covering his face, another bead was found to have been placed inside his mouth. The abundance of jade artefacts can be attributed to the precious nature of the stone; for the ancients, jade represented condensed moisture, including breath, and it is probable that the jade found inside the sarcophagus guaranteed the wearer's continuation of life after death.

Outside the sarcophagus, Ruz found two life-size stucco heads which had been torn from full-length statues located elsewhere at site. The resemblance between these heads and the mosaic mask found in the sarcophagus was striking and led scholars to believe that all of these representations constituted actual portraits of this elite individual. Still, the mystery of his identity wasn't solved until two decades later.

The 1970s represented a watershed in Maya hieroglyphic decipherment. Epigraphers working with the glyphs from Palenque were able to decipher most of the text from the Temple of the Inscriptions. They discovered that much of the information focused on a single person whose name was represented by a miniature Maya war shield. They named this individual 'Pacal', the Maya term for 'shield'. According to the ancient records, Lord Pacal had been born on 26 March 603 to Lady Zac Kuk, a member of one of the ruling families at the site. He acceded to the throne at age 12 in 615, ruling for over 68 years before his death on 31 August 683. It is believed that the 69 steps on the temple's front reflect the fact that Pacal was in his 69th year of rule when he died. According to the texts, the construction of the temple began in 675 and was finally completed in 692, nine years after Pacal's death.

While the texts found throughout the site emphasize events in the life of the

On the oval tablet from the palace at Palenque, Lady Zac K'uk offers her son, Pacal the Great, a headdress of royal authority.

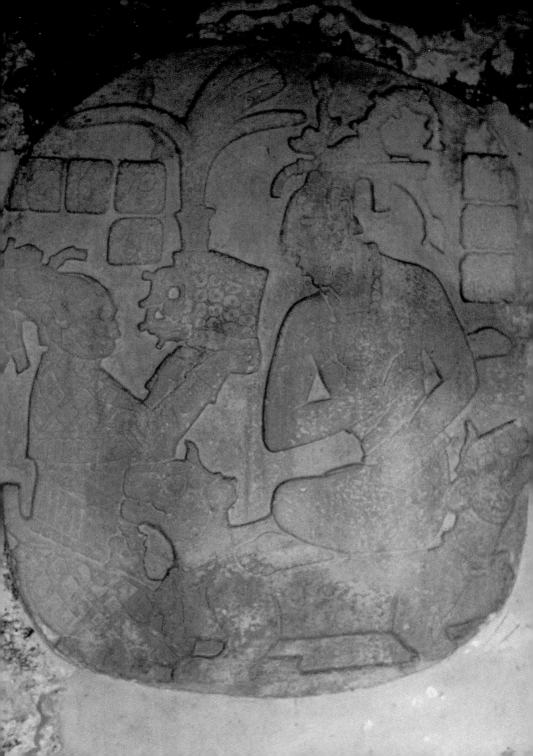

great ruler, the imagery carved into the surfaces of his sarcophagus provides us with insights into his spiritual beliefs. Originally painted red, the monument proclaims Pacal's ascendancy into death and his ancestry. Along the sides of the sarcophagus, the ruler's ancestors emerge from the earth as if to physically support the imagery carved across the lid's surface. On the sarcophagus lid the central image lies within a segmented rectangular border containing celestial symbols and high-ranking nobles. The hieroglyphs making up this 'Celestial Band' are associated with the moon, the sun and the planets Venus and Mars. These symbols place the central figure within a heavenly realm. While Pacal is shown falling into the gaping skeletal maws of the underworld, it was understood that after his descent into Xibalba, the king would rise again and take his place among the stars. A mirror sign, sunk into his forehead, indicates that he is depicted at the moment of his rebirth as a divinity. Jutting out from the mirror is a smoking celt (or axe), an emblem of the serpent-footed God K, a deity who is associated with lineage and the genealogical right to rule.

Pacal's placement in a personified bowl before a stylized tree is a reference to his piety. Bowls such as these were associated with the blood sacrifices offered before trees and monolithic monuments, called stelae. The tree on the sarcophagus lid represents an *axis mundi*, the centre of the world. Like many cultures, the Maya believed that such a 'world tree' stood at the centre of their cosmos. Because its branches reached into the heavens and its roots far down into the earth, this tree provided the deified dead with access into both realms. By displaying himself as a sacrifice placed before the tree, Pacal was indicating his piety and worthiness before the gods.

Because Pacal died before the temple's completion, it was left to his son,

*T**he upper surface of the limestone sarcophagus lid shows Pacal falling into the open maw of the underworld.***

Chan Bahlum ('Serpent Jaguar'), to complete the final phases of the Temple of the Inscription. The new king had ancestors stuccoed into four of the six piers of the temple's façade. As in the case of the sarcophagus lid, the decorated piers are framed by a celestial band indicating that the scenes were spiritually charged. Each figure faces toward the temple's central entrance and holds a small child in his or her arms. On the third pier, Pacal's mother, Lady Zac Kuk, holds a baby who is named as her grandson, Chan Bahlum. The textual evidence is supported by the representation of the child himself, who is shown to have six toes on his left foot. In other representations from Palenque, Chan Bahlum is shown to be polydectile. Beyond showing himself within the context of earlier generations, Chan Bahlum visually connects himself to his father by representing himself as God K. This is indicated by his single serpent foot. Thus, while Pacal's role as an offering before the gods was emphasized within the private space of his crypt, Chan Bahlum's presented himself before the Palencano populace as an incarnation of lineage blood and a legitimate heir to his father's throne.

Across the Otulum, Chan Bahlum continued to emphasize his right as legitimate heir by constructing three small temples: the Temple of the Cross, the Temple of the Foliated Cross and the Temple of the Sun. Shrines within these monuments present Chan Bahlum and his father on either side of a central icon. In the Temple of the Cross, the figures face a stylized world tree with a bird perched atop it. With outstretched arms, Chan Bahlum presents a deity to

*W*ithin the sanctuary of the Temple of the Cross, Chan Bahlum displays a 'Jester God' before a stylized world tree.

*C*han Bahlum's Group of the Cross at Palenque (overleaf) consists of three small temples: the Temple of the Cross, the Temple of the Foliated Cross and the Temple of the Sun.

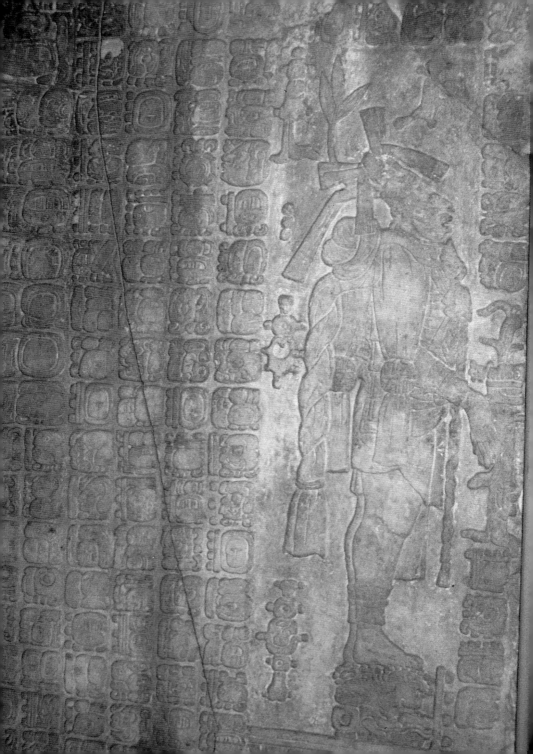

*O*n the left side of the cross, the deceased Pacal holds a quadripartite god. The foliage behind the king's head may refer to his status as a divine ancestor.

*C*han Bahlum holds the emblem of lineage blood, God K, in his upraised hand. The deity is marked here by the smoking celt protruding from his head.

the tree, while Pacal, dressed in burial garments, holds a miniature replica of a personified offering bowl. Heraldic representation such as this has precedence in the early imagery of Hunahpu and Xbalanque, the Hero Twins of the *Popol Vuh*, the Quiche Maya Book of Genesis. Although this myth is 2,000 years old it was only recorded into European script after the Conquest. In one episode from this primordial tale, the protagonists are able to re-establish world order by shooting the vain supernatural bird, Vucub Caquix, from his perch atop a tree. Since one of the functions of Maya rulers was to maintain order on behalf of their people, it is not at all surprising that we see Chan Bahlum and Pacal take up the positions of the Hero Twins before the tree .

Copán, Honduras

Far from Palenque, Copán is situated in a valley on the Copán River in northern Honduras. For over 400 years this ancient city and the surrounding environs were under the control of a single dynasty. The first of the rulers, Yax Kuk Mo ('Blue-Quetzal-Macaw'), established his rule during the 5th century AD. Huge

*T*he Copán River, situated next to the acropolis at Copán, was the main source of water for the metropolis during the Classic Period.

*S tone head
from the
acropolis, Copán.*

*T*he east face of Stele C, Copán, in the centre of the ceremonial court. This is a double figure, facing both east and west.

*S*ixteen kings flank the sides of Altar Q, Copán. On the front, Yax Pac accepts a staff of authority from the linear progenitor, Yax Kuk Mo. Each sits on a hieroglyph of his name.

*S*tele H, from Copán, depicts 18-Rabbit in his guise as First Father, a primordial creator god.

*T*he stone known as the 'Old Man of Copán' was part of an 'atlantean' figure supporting one of the corners of a temple atop the acropolis at the site.

pyramids, stelae and altars scattered across the site's five plazas spectacularly proclaim the successful war campaigns and histories of subsequent Copánec rulers. For example, the Hieroglyphic Stairway, containing the longest inscription in the New World, records the accessions of each of the kings up to the reign of the fourteenth ruler. Pedestals, placed at equidistant intervals along the central axis of the stairway, support life-size sculptures of five of the kings. Each figure is shown in war-associated regalia, an indication of prowess as a great warrior. Another monument, Altar Q, portrays all 16 rulers of the site around its parameter. On the front of the altar, Yax Kuk Mo is shown handing the sceptre of authority to his descendent Yax Pac, the last great ruler of the site. On the top of this monument, the text underlines Yax Pac's legitimacy as a ruler by referencing the reign of the earliest dynast.

The Ruler 18-Rabbit

One of the most famous of the Copanec rulers, 18-Rabbit, was the subject of many of the massive stelae located in the Great Plaza. Collectively, these monuments function as a kind of symbolic forest and are referred to in their texts as *te-tunob* ('tree-stones'). Each bears the image of 18-Rabbit in the guise of a deity . On Stela D, dated to 736 AD, 18-Rabbit wears the mask of the Sun God. An oblong 'reflection sign' sunk into his forehead implies that, in this guise, the ruler took on the resplendent nature of the sun itself. This artistic format not only emphasized the semi-divine quality of the king but also his role as a living manifestation of the *axis mundi*. As was befitting all world trees, offerings would be placed on altars positioned before these tree-stones.

18-Rabbit was also responsible for the Great Ballcourt, one of the largest

playing fields ever produced by the Maya. Although the exact rules of the game have been obscured by time, it is known that the event involved many players who tried to advance a rubber ball down the I-shaped field. From the imagery associated with such courts, it is also clear that the game held religious significance. According to the *Popol Vuh*, Hunahpu and Xbalanque, were the first ballplayers. When their noisy playing disturbed the lords of the underworld, they were summoned before the deities to atone for their disrespect. As the story goes, the twins survived their punishments, eventually defeated the evil deities and were reborn as the sun and the moon. It is possible that players who lost this game were sacrificed and believed to have gone to Xibalba. There, like the twins, they would play the game for amusement of the lords of the underworld and also deliver messages from their king.

Before important events, ritual autosacrifice was performed in of shrines within temples. The entrance to Temple 22 took the form of the open maw of a gigantic earth monster. Crossing over the tooth-lined threshold, the king

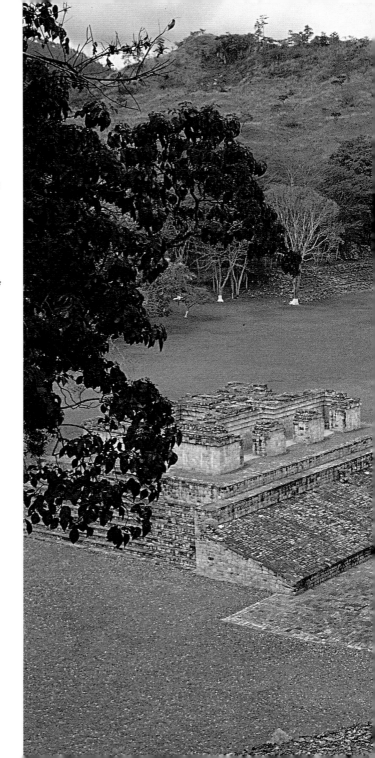

*T*he ballgame played
on the surface of
the ballcourt at Copán
not only invoked ancient
mythology, but could
have deadly consequences
for the players.

*The maw-shaped portal
of Copán's Temple 22
conceptually marked the
inner sanctuary as a cave in
a great symbolic mountain.*

would symbolically enter into a world cave. The lintel of the interior shrine represents the body of a deer-headed Celestial Monster. Its torso is defined by tiny ancestors swimming amidst streams of S-shaped blood. The head and tail of the Celestial Monster are supported by Pauahtunob, creatures responsible for holding up the sky at its four corners. After making his blood sacrifice inside of this sacred space, the ruler was able to communicate with and honour his ancestors.

Whereas 18-Rabbit's architectural campaigns were primarily focused on the northern part of the site, the monuments of Yax Pac, the last ruler of the site, were in the southern part. Both the East and West Courts symbolically represent Xibalban ballcourts. In the West Court, the flat playing field is demarcated by three square ballcourt markers bearing visages of God K. The king and his courtiers watched the play from an elevated 'reviewing stand'. At either end of the stand, anthropomorphic monkeys hold torches with a T-shaped

The head of God III, a jaguarian deity associated with Venus, is located in the centre of the East Court stairs at Copán.

The back of stele H from Copán.

Ik signs, symbols of life and the wind. This may refer to the wind and rain-bringing clouds which were perceived to come from the cave openings. The watery nature of the underworld is indicated by the presence of God I, a fish-associated deity, and by the carved conch shells situated before him.

Likewise, the East Court had ballcourt markers indicating a playing field. Its central figure was the brother of God I, God III, a jaguar-associated deity. The W-shaped Venus signs flanking his face refer to God III's association with the planet, Venus. His placement in the East Court is significant inasmuch as Venus, in its form as morning star, was believed to pull the sun up out of the

underworld. At either end of the reviewing stand, rampant jaguars dance out of Xibalba. Their now-hollow spots once held obsidian inlay which would reflect the rising sun as it was reborn each day – a fitting reception for so important a giver of life.

Sometime during the 8th century AD, Maya sites all over Mesoamerica began to collapse. Many theories have been suggested for the abandonment of the great cities – ecological disaster, war and famine are but a few. At the site of Copán, the impending calamity is reflected in the last monuments of Yax Pac. Temple 18, Yax Pac's mortuary temple, is one of the smallest constructions at the site and stands in stark contrast to the massive monuments produced by his great ancestors. On each of its four interior piers, Yax Pac presented himself as a great warlord, wielding shield and spear and dressed in cotton armour. With the collapse of the site immanent, his attire may have reflected internal and external strife. Without supporting texts, however, it may never be known if this is an accurate portrayal of Yax Pac's capabilities as a warrior or simply wishful thinking on the part of a ruler witnessing the decline of this great city and civilization.

Y ax Pac's last construction, Temple 18, was probably built as the ruler's final resting place. His image is located on the four internal piers of the complex.

THE
MAYAN
ENIGMA

PHOTOGRAPHIC ACKNOWLEDGEMENTS
Cover Merle Green Robertson [MGR];
pp. 2–3 AKG London; pp. 5, 6–7 Pictures of
Record [PR]; pp. 8–9 MGR;
pp. 10, 11 Werner Forman; p. 13 PR;
p. 14 MGR; pp. 16, 18–19, 20, 21 PR;
p. 22–3 Constance Cortez [CC];
pp.24–5, 26, 26–7 Peter Clayton [PC];
pp. 28, 29 Andrea Stone; p. 30, 31 CC;
pp.32–3 PC; pp.34–5, 36 CC;
p. 37 Andrea Stone; p. 38 CC.

First published in Great Britain 1997
by George Weidenfeld and Nicolson Ltd
The Orion Publishing Group
5 Upper St Martin's Lane
London WC2H 9EA

A CIP catalogue record for this book is available
from the British Library
ISBN 0 297 823078

Picture Research: Joanne King

Designed by Harry Green

Typeset in Baskerville